# Underground River of Want

*poems by*

# Kathleen Gregg

*Finishing Line Press*
Georgetown, Kentucky

# Underground River of Want

Copyright © 2021 by Kathleen Gregg
ISBN 978-1-64662-599-4 First Edition
All rights reserved under International and Pan-American Copyright Conventions. No part of this book may be reproduced in any manner whatsoever without written permission from the publisher, except in the case of brief quotations embodied in critical articles and reviews.

## ACKNOWLEDGMENTS

My gratitude goes to the editors of the following journals, in which poems in this book, sometimes in earlier versions, first appeared:

*Ghost City Review:* "The Round Table at Buddha Lounge"
*Gyroscope Review, The Crone Issue*: "Changing My Religion"
*Highland Park Poetry, Driving Cars Anthology*: "Sometimes Freedom Is a '93 Dodge Shadow"
*Pegasus*: "Food, Post-Divorce," "Aubade"
*Memoir Mixtape*, Vol. 12: "Everything Has Changed"
*Literary Accents Magazine*, Issue #4: "One-Thirty, A.M.," "Jumping the Fence"

My humble thanks go to Jeff Worley, Poet Laureate of Kentucky, 2019-2020, who mentored me with patience and a wonderful sense of humor for close to a year. Through his eyes, I began to actually see myself as a poet. Thanks also to my Buddha Girls and fellow poets, Sylvia, Shelda, Mary and Debbie, who continually encourage, support and inspire me. Many thanks to Sherry Chandler, her brilliant mind, and the way she has challenged me to get out of my comfort zone during the numerous poetry-writing classes I have taken from her at Carnegie Center in Lexington. And a special shout-out to Katerina Stoykova, whose insight and direction was so valuable to me in assembling this chapbook.

Publisher: Leah Huete de Maines
Editor: Christen Kincaid
Cover Art: "S'il Vous Plait" by Elizabeth Heichelbech
Author Photo: Charlie Gregg
Cover Design: Elizabeth Maines McCleavy

Order online: www.finishinglinepress.com
also available on amazon.com

Author inquiries and mail orders:
Finishing Line Press
PO Box 1626
Georgetown, Kentucky 40324
USA

# Table of Contents

January, 1964 ............................................................................. 1

The Young Girl Mourns Alone ................................................. 2

Father-Less ................................................................................ 3

The Eve Syndrome .................................................................... 5

Heartbreak Is A Winter Wind .................................................. 6

Winter Incantation ................................................................... 7

Spring Street Bar, NYC ............................................................ 8

One-Thirty, A.M. ...................................................................... 9

Emergence ............................................................................... 10

Jumping The Fence ................................................................. 12

Everything Has Changed ........................................................ 13

Food, Post Divorce .................................................................. 14

Sometimes Freedom Is A '93 Dodge Shadow ....................... 16

Charlie's Invitation ................................................................. 17

Fire And Light ......................................................................... 18

Along For The Ride ................................................................ 19

Changing My Religion ............................................................ 20

How Odds Change ................................................................. 21

The Round Table At Buddha Lounge .................................... 22

Aubade ..................................................................................... 23

Rolling With The Stones ........................................................ 24

*For Charlie,*
*who never stops believing in me*

## JANUARY 1964

The paramedics strap my dad
onto the stretcher and wheel him
out to the waiting ambulance. *It's*

*probably pancreatitis.* Their edgy voices
telegraph worry, amplify
the tension tightening around us.

A cold tug of alarm shivers
through my body. My sister gathers me in.
Unasked questions are swallowed, churn

in my stomach for one terrible week. Until,
the dreaded call from mom; a bedside
summons that wrenches

the two of us from sleep, lays bare
the panic choking mom's voice. The dark
drive to the hospital lashes us together:

me, my sister, our fear;
the radio pleading,
                    *I wanna hold your hand.*

## THE YOUNG GIRL MOURNS ALONE

my dad's death   slams into me   like a sudden   howling   wind

that rips my roots   from the ground   severs
                                                        my heart

the shadow of my mom   sweeps   across the wreckage
                                                        and retreats

she won't   look back

I can't   see forward   can't   claw my way
                                         upright

sorrow   leafs out   brown and crushing   like the silence in our house

I am   the splintered limb   nobody wants
                                             to lift up

my pillow   accepts my tears   my closet   gathers me close
                                                                rocks me

my dad   slips into my dreams   I run to him   he scoops me up

that joy   that deliverance   from grief

awake   I am as much a ghost as he is   I keep waiting for him

to walk in the door   and call out
                                *Where's my little Kit?*
and where am I?

## FATHER-LESS

1.
grief   is a thick corona
surrounding me
an energy   that repels people

at school   eyes shift away
            smiles
are tight-lipped   forced

at home   we are planets
            in separate orbit
around Dad's death   comfort
skitters off   dodges
my dark matter

my body
        is an underground river
                of want
someone   please   touch   me

2.
*I will touch you*, the boy's eyes
            promise
his slow graze
up and down my body
                stirs
a deep belly thrill
            heats my face

        the boy smiles
        asks me out

no father to tell me no

3.
can the end of innocence
be measured in miles     how long
is the sneak

from my house to his

      bed

summer mornings
parents at work
my body
        slick
             with guilt

4.
*I don't want to do this anymore*
      finally    I say it
search    the boy's eyes for
his    professed love
               find lowered lids
*you know this means we break up*
such easy dismissal
              ricochets
through my body    slaps    me    awake
      shames    me

      the boy frowns
      walks away

and now    there is no me    just
      the impression
his fingers have left
             on my skin

## THE EVE SYNDROME

We can't go back, can we,
to easy lightness.  Hand
floating out the car window,
cupping the air currents; joy
so reachable.  Before

his devout white collar,
his too handsome face
full of kind concern.
Comfort quoted from scripture,
while his eyes offered
more and more.  Before

conversations turned to flirt,
skirted the subject of desire,
allowed youthful fantasies
to ripen.  Before

his visits stopped; temptation
the hinted-at reason.  Blame
coiled around a heart.
Before

the dragging weight
of secret shame.  Hand
slapped down.

## HEARTBREAK IS A WINTER WIND

    it blows like the downward lash
    of a whip on bare flesh
                      deep sting
            lacerating hope

    it blows like the fat flat of a palm
    shoving you backwards
                      flailing
            failing to recover equilibrium

    it blows like a shrill scream of hatred
            like the howl of a caged dog

    it blows like the stiff straw
    of a broom
           sweeping
                      the dust of love away

# WINTER INCANTATION

Rise up Winter

skin tree limbs black   freeze their sap   lick the last drops
dredge grass of its green   harden the earth beneath
smear the sky gray   smother days with stolen light
embolden night   to whistle and whine at our windows

Storm us Winter

rage gales   of sideways sleet and flurry
bend our backs   against your cold shove
thread needles   of raw sting   down our necks
glaze roads   into mirrored menace
spin and skid   impotent tire treads
spill cars   helpless   into ditches

Dazzle us Winter

frost our lawns   with layers of white   spritzed light
cling candles   of up-side-down ice   to our eaves
blaze them   with reflected sunfire
glitter and gleam and glint   squint our eyes
snowglobe your silhouette   soften the conversation
summon snowmen   angel wings   powdered breath

## SPRING STREET BAR, NYC

He chooses David Bowie's *Changes,* says
*This is our song, Babe*
                          leans close   sings softly
my body heat   remembers
the makeshift platform bed waiting
back at his artists' commune

*One of the guys who lives here was Janis Joplin's lover,*
he'd told me
reckless   thrilling
                      just like this impetuous trip

    just like the time

I popped myself out of my boyfriend's sunroof
            naked    from the waist up
one clear   moon-glossed night   and rode
the back roads of my little hometown
letting the wind
                taste my skin

under the table   I lay my hand
on his inner thigh   slowly glide my way up   brush
    across his lap
his sharp inhale
the lightning in his glance   charges   my senses
                    must be love
he's already said it is

he leads me
through the crowded bar to the door
I stroke his back
               with my body
                        want
nothing to do with the pain pouring out
of the jukebox   Billie Holiday
*Good Morning Heartache*

## ONE-THIRTY A.M.

The train rattles the windows,
and I wait.

> the bars closed at 1:00
> he's settled up the tab
> short drive home
> and right on cue

my husband staggers in the door, lurches
through the dark house, stumbles over

the threshold to our bedroom; work clothes
tugged off and slung into the corner.

He yanks back the covers, thuds onto the bed.
A bitter tang of sweat, cigarette smoke and beer billows up.

Hands grope me, rub along my thigh.
I shove his arms away.

He slurs
*What's your problem?*
I  s c r e a m
the answer in my head.

But he's already passed out. Again. And again,
It's the train that I'm left with. The sound of leaving

settles in my bones. *When?* the whistle asks.
*When?*

## EMERGENCE

1.

She has broken through the loam,
urged upward
by waiting sunlight
and just the right timing.
She is freed;
her promise unburied
and opening
into velveteen petals bright
with unabashed color.


2.

Nothing is that simple, of course.
The wind swirls with forces
that test her stem strength.
She risks being thwarted
by choking weeds,
by raging rain,
by her own temptation
to sink back down
into familiar dark
suspension.

3.

She dreams of reaching
full bloom
on her own terms:
never cut short,
never stuffed into a vase,
trapped and wilting.


4.

Dreams are just the start.

## JUMPING THE FENCE

Another job lost, the King of Drama
held out a gun I didn't know he owned,

begged me to hide it. Suicide
was the shadowy threat

his eyes couldn't quite fake.
I stared at his outstretched arm,

felt the final knot fray,
the tether snap,

and remembered
the German Shepherd next door;

silent and shivering, water
in his bowl frozen. When

he finally jumped the fence,
I cheered. Elation is the flip side

of fear. My trembling hands stack
the last load into the U-haul:

jazz albums, hiking boots, Matisse print,
pink toolbox, wedding china, sheer

will power. This is it. My fingers grip
the cold courage of the steering wheel,

every nerve in my body springs
alive.

## EVERYTHING HAS CHANGED

Regret is a raw nerve throbbing
so close to the surface it glares
between blinks of my eyes, trembles
my glass of scotch. I beg your ghosting
of me to *stop  please  stop*  singing
softly in my ear like I used to love
when we slow danced in the living room,
kids asleep. Before our falter, before
failure, finally. And when

will it stop? This love hunkered down
on a Saturday night and I am alone,
listening to Nina Simone pierce my heart;
aching with her as she propels her pain
across the piano keys,
hands and voice a single vessel
that careens me to the edge.

Exactly, Nina, exactly.

*Note: This title is a reference to Everything Must Change,
sung by Nina Simone*

## FOOD, POST DIVORCE

peanut butter slathered
on sliced apples
soda crackers on the side
fried egg sandwiches
boxed macaroni and cheese
various frozen dinners
my ex would call it
*junk food*   not fit for dinner

we ate my home cooking
for twenty-one years   now
I read a book until my stomach
rumbles a reminder to eat
when   and what   I want
and by the way
I call it *food I can afford*

I'm vegetarian by necessity
except the few times I splurge
(after vivid carnivorous dreams)
on a succulent rotisserie chicken
devoured over my kitchen sink
sans silverware
stuffing the juicy meat
the herb-crusted skin
into my mouth
grease dripping down my chin

I pick every last morsel
of meat off the bone   recycle
into chicken noodle soup

several nights a week
fifteen-minute break
PayDay candy bar
gulped down
peanuts equal protein
second job equals paid phone bill
gas money   freedom

I call it *food I can't afford
to do without*

## SOMETIMES FREEDOM IS A '93 DODGE SHADOW

Boxy, khaki green, low-end model
fully equipped
with rolldown windows,
with one of its keys permanently stuck
in the ignition,
and with two years left on the loan.
I call it my consolation prize
for losing at marriage.
But damn, that Dodge is everything
my ex-husband is not.

When I unlock the driver's side door,
I know I will be sliding
into basic, snug comfort.
My choice of radio station
doesn't need to be justified,
or mean another option
isn't good enough.
I am never troubled
by temperature ups and downs.
My Shadow always starts,
always takes me where I want to go
under the radar,
the road reimagined.

## CHARLIE'S INVITATION

Come glide with me
through the cool, still waters

of the river.  Listen to the lullaby
of oars upon the surface,

smooth and rhythmic, stroking
us forward.  The sun will gift us

with skin soaking warmth, glitter
the sweat beaded upon our bodies.

Our vibrations in tandem, rippling
outward, will sound an alarm

to the long-legged heron grazing
for minnows in pools by the river bank.

And she will take flight:
expanse of wing against lapis sky,

a lavish sweep across the palisades.
Later, we will drift with oars suspended

to within yards of motionless turtles
sunbathing on a fallen tree limb.

They will startle and splash
at the sound of our laughter, as we

sip cold wine from a mason jar,
as we sway in gentle waters.

## FIRE AND LIGHT

Cedar logs in the woodstove burn
blue-hot.  Flames sway and shimmy,
dance with shadows.  Dawn's light is spare,
shrouded in gray.  Strands of mist hover
outside the window, like ghosts.

Beneath a blanket, we lie entwined;
charmed by the spark and hiss of fire,
by the spectral light.  We linger
at the edge of wakefulness and dreams.
Our hands seek bare skin, capture
and surrender heat.  Desire blazes,
burns blue-hot.

## ALONG FOR THE RIDE
*(Jessamine County, Kentucky)*

I watch our shadow ride along next to us,
projected against the old stone fences
like a silent movie flickering in and out
of the tangled foliage screening
the edge of the road. Two sets of phantom
legs peddle in perfect syncopation,
in the easy rhythm between Charlie and me
on our tandem bike. Mirages shimmer

above the seared pavement. Sweat glistens
our skin, soaks our jerseys. Shade smoothed
across the road feels like a cool shower.
Our shadow paces us past an old curing barn,
where the dry-leaf aroma of tobacco lingers;
past a newly mown field flecked with rounds

of baled hay. Then it's two remaining hills
and the last flat sprint to our house. We roll
up the driveway and settle to a stop, our feet
hitting the ground simultaneously. We are
smooth, practiced precision. We are
each other's shadow.

## CHANGING MY RELIGION

Everything changes.
My long love affair with the sun
has ended.  Age and skin cancer
have soured me, cowered me
under layers of cotton, straw hats,
sunblock.  I laugh

at how much I now resemble
my mother's cousin, Louisa, who was
a Mennonite.  True to the teachings,
she always wore plain black,
long sleeved, ankle length dresses,
probably homemade,
black lace-up boots
and a sun bonnet tied
under her chin.  Witch-like,
in my imagination, even though
she would smile and joke with my mom
as we strolled down the rows
of her neatly tended garden,
picking green beans,
or asparagus, or cantaloupe,
or strawberries.  Still, I felt thankful

that my family was Methodist.
Mom wasn't about to hide
her light under a bushel.  She wore
bright, flower printed sundresses,
a string of pearls at her neck
and red lipstick.  As a kid, that choice
couldn't have been clearer.

Seems the devil was in the flash.

## HOW ODDS CHANGE

Like leaning against the fence in the paddock area,
watching the number seven horse toss his head,
fight the reins, all that tight energy.
The only gray in the race.  30-1 long shot.
I'm too jittery to place even a $6.00 bet,
and disgusted with myself when he wins -
almost my car payment!  Years later,

I attend an artist's reception, single out
a painting that keeps drawing my eye:
pastel rendering of a jockey atop his horse,
the trainer still holding the reins.
Part impressionist, part abstract, part cubist.
It has soft intimacy, bold orange accents.
The artist is describing how she hangs out
at Keeneland Racetrack, trying to catch
the right pose, the right light;
how she tries to convey emotion
using the angle and curve of her lines.
She can see how taken I am with the piece,
senses her odds for a sale are good.
I bet on myself.
And tonight, we both win.

## THE ROUND TABLE AT BUDDHA LOUNGE

Post lunch rush,
Buddha Lounge morphs
into our own private dining room.
Writers, we serve up language
as delicious to us
as the wasabi-infused soy sauce,
shaved ginger,
sweet chili shrimp,
Korean tacos, sushi.
As nourishing

as our Edward Hopper view:
The narrow, one-way slant
of Mill Street wedging cars
into metered parking slots.
A curbside row of dumpsters,
New York City style,
spoiling the storefront
of Goodfella's Pizza.
An aproned cook leaning
against one of two outdoor tables
and smoking.
A trickle of pedestrians
trafficking by.

This place inspires us.  Ideas
are chopsticked into our mouths,
chewed up and swallowed.  Laughter
drops onto our laps.  We pat
our lips with weaves of poetry.

We are hip and we know it;
retired professional women
exploring new menus.
Age is incidental.  It just pays
the tip.

## AUBADE

light still clings to the crescent moon
pale opalescence
on the brink
of losing its fire

aromas of wood smoke
damp crushed leaves
funnel
through my cracked window

I slip outdoors
into the cool on my face
the lush hush of dawn hanging
like a pause between breaths

Charlie slides up behind me
warm lips nuzzle my neck
we linger on the porch
seasoning our day

a distant train whistle
is the echo of commerce
far-off destinations
unstoppable movement

allure that has drifted
away from us
days of deadlines
left behind

Charlie gathers my hand in his
smiles
as the sun flashes
first light

## ROLLING WITH THE STONES

1967
*Between the Buttons,*
first album I ever bought.
Bluesy rock and roll,
scandalous lyrics, irresistible.
I have it still:
torn cover, scratched vinyl,
permanent patina of spilled beer.

Saturday night, mom on a date,
my living room is the dance floor.
We smuggle in liquor bought
with fake IDs.
The party isn't over until
we dance to the whole album,
in a circle of frenzied, free-form
movement; then collapse
into a heap, laughing.  Cheers
to Mick!
our bad boy,
our uninhibited howl,
our alter ego.

1978
Rupp Arena, the *Some Girls Tour*,
quite a coup for Lexington, Kentucky.
Sold out in minutes. Seats
behind the stage are offered.
Hundreds of us snatch them up.

My sister-in-law and I, both big
with baby, are conspicuous
in a surging mass of decked-out
female fans. Our husbands eye
their flat, sexy stomachs
with longing. Forget that.
When the band takes the stage,
we two mommas are on our feet,
bellies bobbing, shouting *no thanks*
to the joint being passed down the aisle.

Almost every song, Mick turns around
and sings to us, the backdoor crowd.
Call and response. We are drenched
in his energy.

2016
*Blue and Lonesome,*
Back to their roots.  Recorded
on the fly.  Most tracks
not rehearsed, just played
from the gut; the Blues being
a genre where age is an asset.

Christmas day, Charlie and I sip wine,
drowse in the heat of our woodstove.
In lieu of carols, we opt
for the Stones; their new CD
a surprise in my stocking.
And oh hell yes,
heartache is wailed
in a voice unfiltered and raw.
You tell it, Mick!
The story isn't over.

**Kathleen Gregg** lives with her husband and one cat in the beautiful Bluegrass region of Kentucky, where storytelling is as much a tradition as horse racing and bourbon distilling are. She mentored by Jeff Worley, 2019-2020 Kentucky Poet Laureate, for a year, through the Author Academy program at Carnegie Center for Literacy and Learning in Lexington. She is a member of the Kentucky State Poetry Society, currently serving as treasurer. Her poems have been published in *Lady Literary Journal, Gyroscope Review, Workhorse, Highland Park Poetry, Literary Accents Magazine,* among others. This is her first chapbook.

www.ingramcontent.com/pod-product-compliance
Lightning Source LLC
LaVergne TN
LVHW041518070426
835507LV00012B/1652